Michael J. Leach's *Chords in the Soundscapes* is a polyphonic delight. His work is a poetic album of visual, sonic, and narrative compositions that weaves history, science, and theory into powerful emotive articulation. Leach is a textured storyteller with inventive phrasing. Make sure you bathe in sunlight as you curl up on the couch, drop an (imagined) stylus on *Chords in the Soundscapes*, and press play.

Alicia Sometimes

More than a tribute to song, *Chords in the Soundscapes* moves us through music, science, art, confession, numbers, space, and time. Michael J. Leach is a poet 'dabbling in eternalism', sharing his playlist of connection and loss, waves of sound and light rendered through the prism of language. The philosopher Simon Critchley says: 'We are mystics when we're listening to the music we love.' Leach has always seemed to know this.

Nathan Curnow

Chords
in the
Soundscapes

Michael J. Leach

This poetry collection is dedicated to: my mother, Judy Leach (1953-2020), who loved soul music; my maternal grandmother, Lily Wheeler (1923-2012), who loved the bagpipes; my maternal grandfather, Eric Wheeler (1927-2016), who was a country music singer and guitarist; my paternal grandparents, Hilary Leach (1929-2025) and Roy Leach (1928-1993), who ran Roy Leach Music Centre.

This poetry collection is also dedicated to the memory and legacy of Stephen Matthews OAM (1946-2024), who ran Ginninderra Press from 1996 to 2024 and who selected *Chords in the Soundscapes* for publication in November 2023.

Chords in the Soundscapes
ISBN 978 1 76109 928 1
Copyright © text Michael J. Leach 2025
Typesetting by Rack and Rune Publishing
Cover Design by Graham Davidson based on a photograph supplied by Michael J. Leach, *Sheet Music in the Wind*

First published 2025 by
GINNINDERRA PRESS
PO Box 2 Bentleigh 3204
ginninderrapress.com.au

Music is ekphrastic poetry
we draw on our own experiences
to understand who we are
who we want to be

Brenda Eldridge,
'Ekphrastic Poetry', *Sounds & Silences*, 2023

Only emotion endures

Ezra Pound,
Literary Essays of Ezra Pound, 1968

There is a Spotify playlist of songs and pieces of music that are referred to, or alluded to, in the poems throughout this collection: https://open.spotify.com/playlist/7bN1s9PUYipxP4pKakkPtg

Contents

Part 1: The Science of Music	9
Stage Shows	11
Music Shop Memories	14
Day of the Sun	16
Emergence of Voice	18
Imagined Piano Lessons	22
Acoustics	24
Jazz-al	25
Wind Chimes	26
Pre-Reformation Tea Party	27
One Halloween	28
Dolphins	29
(Mis)pronunciation	31
(H)ear	33
She Who Rocks	34
(Im)mortal Coils	35
Uamh Bhin, or The Melodious Cave	36
Numerology	38
Two Branches	39
Music Critics Tread a Fine Line	41
Traversing the Soundscapes	42
Golden Satellite	46
Blue Thought	48
First Dance	54
Applied Neuroscience	55
Sheepwash Creek Ginko	56
Well-being	57
Closer	59
Sliding and Rising	60
Stress-soothing Songs	62

Trajectory	64
Fluidal	66
Khronos	68
I Recall When the Kind ICU Staff Kept Calm	70
Intermission	71
in the hospital chapel	72
Part 2: Love Notes	73
The Warmth of Her Light	75
Life Symbol	76
Mum's Life and Death Song	77
December Remembrances of the Worst Winter	78
Twenty-Six Things I Remember about My Mother	81
Gratitunes	82
Quintet	83
Familial	84
Over the Rainbow	86
Lily	88
Grandpa's Acoustic Guitar	89
Elvis	93
Temporelle	94
Armchair Travelling in January 2021	96
A Pastoral for Nate & Damien	97
Lovecats Triolet	98
Roxette Triolet	99
Triple J Hottest 100 2022 Votes (In Poetic Order)	100
Trees	101
Seasonal Migration	104
The Plight of the Adélie Penguin	105
Non-human Nature	106

(Sym)phonic	108
Musical Styles	110
the story	111
Playlist	112
My Treasure	114
Two Weeks Together	116
Between Strathfieldsaye & Speers Point	119
Apple-esque, or You're Like My First Celebrity Crush But Better	120
Enshrined	121
Falls	124
Steel City	125
Philology	127
Reindeer	130
Somewhere on Awabakal Country	132
Acknowledgements	134
About the Author	136

Part 1

The Science of Music

Stage Shows

My beloved mother was a lifelong fan
          of the Godfather
of Soul, James Brown.

Mum rarely repeated the same anecdote
but, when it came to James Brown, she was happy
to entertain an exception.

Periodically, she'd share this striking story
of seeing & hearing James Brown perform live
          with characteristic vigour
          & multiphonic vocals
on stage at a venue in Berlin

way back when she worked back
stage at said German venue
in the name of big names like James Brown,
all thanks to a working holiday visa
circa 1973.

I can still picture that enthused expression
on Mum's eternally youthful face –
the countenance of a schoolkid recounting
a short tale from a summertime sojourn.

She'd take off on a retelling punctuated
by the reassuringly familiar words
To cut a long story
short.

This particular story would always end
on the same notes
on that same set of singular images:

the image
of James Brown
repeatedly dropping to his knees
between the band and the audience
towards the end of his extended set
like some ultramarathon runner
approaching their physical limit

the image
of James Brown's
best bandmate cloaking James Brown
in a cape before taking him off
stage, as though the chorus
to his biggest hit
'I Feel Good' didn't ring as true as it could

the image
of James Brown
running back on stage
flinging his cape to the floor
and performing with renewed vigour
like some phantom resurrected & reenergised

the image
of a young woman – my mother –
seeing & hearing James Brown's encore
from stage right
while forming lifelong memories.

When I retell my beloved mother's anecdote
about the Godfather of Soul, James Brown,
with or without my own spin
of figurative flourishes,
I can't help but feel

Mum reminds me of James Brown –
they were both beyond reluctant
to leave.

Music Shop Memories

I still remember
my paternal grandparents'
independent music
shop

in the midst of my hometown –
the one deep in that Beehive
Building, down its dusky
walkway separating one mall   from another.

I have yellowed memories
of stands brimful
of sheet music
that I could've read   but rarely did.

I have yellowed memories
of stands brimful
of strings
that I would've broken   if I'd strummed them
      enough.

I have yellowed memories
of walls brimful
of various chordophones
that I couldn't play   properly.

I have yellowed memories
of aisles brimful
of people browsing buying chatting
longer than they would've   elsewhere.

I have a yellowed heart
-string that still vibrates
at constant frequencies
for the couple of jovial
owners who personned   the front counter.

Day of the Sun

*after 'Now and Then' (*Sumo, EastWest/Warner, 1998*) by The Superjesus*

After my phone alarm,
I open dimmed eyes
rise with violin & cello strings
then walk
to the beat of another's drums
to the rhythm of others' guitars.

Sarah McLeod's vocalisations
quell memories of nightmares
by sweetening the morning air
like the birdsong –
those towering, tinkering trills –
of the superb fairy-wren.

As I take my first sip
of milky, morning coffee,
I wonder: does that band name
The Superjesus
actually mean above Jesus?

As Sarah sings about another dawn,
I taste toasted muesli
and decide the answer doesn't matter
because, either way, hearing
her alt-rock band play
'Now and Then'
is a religious experience.

After the diminuendo,
                        the crescendo
compels me out the front door
into gathering daylight,
the vocalist, band
and Adelaide Symphony Orchestra
forming an ensemble of fiery seraphim.

Feeling transient yet transcendent,
I surrender my skin & my sins
to the radiance of sunlight.

Emergence of Voice

i've
always
been shy

my
20th-
century
memories

        encompass
                bro   ken
                       moments:

                            the lights
                            go out
                            in my room –
                            i pull bedding
                            over my face
                            & feel
                            safe

                            the door
                            bell rings –
                            i run to Mum's side
                            & then slide
                            beneath
                            the daybed

                      schoolkids stare
                      at bespectacled eyes –
                      i hang my head
                      low
                      & speak
                      to precious few

                      the school stage
                      show –
                      i stand
                      to one side
                      & shine lights
                      on stars

i've
always
been shy

my
21st-
century
memories

        encompass
            breakthrough
                moments:

lights shine
on me –
I stand alone
on the stage
& recite
another's words

new kids look
at me –
I establish
eye contact
& speak
to them too

the final siren
sounds
– I high
five teammates
& shake
hands with rivals

the lights
go out
in my room –
I wrap myself
in ghosts
& feel
safe

i've
always
been shy

        yet   now
        somehow

                I stand up
                    in front
            of health care students
                    to teach
                them how
                to care

i've
always
been shy

        yet   now
        somehow

                I stand up
                    at weddings
                    & funerals
                to recite
            my free
              verse

Imagined Piano Lessons

Sometimes I imagine
I'd continued piano lessons
beyond primary school.
I imagine
that the upright piano
        in the dining room
were more than a dusty ornament.
I imagine
that, each December,
I'd play classical Christmas carols
                like Leontovych's
'Carol of the Bells'
                Mendelssohn's
'Hark! The Herald Angels Sing'
                & von Bingen's
'O Frondens Virga'.
I imagine
that, each other month,
I'd play non-classical tunes
                like Alicia
Keys' 'Fallin''
                Regina
Spektor's 'Fidelity'
                & John
Lennon's 'Imagine'.

Sometimes I imagine
I'd somehow always
had the vocal power, the projection
the modulation
to sing along with the strung
soundboard.

Acoustics

sometimes
i get dis-
tract-
ed
by cacophonies of contemporary sounds –
traffic noise thru single-glazed glass
white noise from white goods
new playlists of sad songs
all my <u>curses</u> & <u>sighs</u>
finger taps on keys
~~background~~ TV
and so on…
i just get
so dis-
tract-
ed
by cacophonies of contemporary sounds
that i'm deafened
to those symphonies   of timeless sounds –
the sunny songs of birdlife
the rhythms of resting…breaths
the rustling leaves of brilliant books
the resonance of didgeridoos and bagpipes
the anti-venom in the voices of those who'd build

                          me   up   up   up –
                                          beyond
                          the deci-
                  bels of
          venom
      -ous
   self-
talk

Jazz-al

I've always been so geeky, awkward and all that, well, jazz.
The bullies at school dropped me to nine circles of hell, Jazz.

I thought you were as cool as Princess Jazz from *Aladdin*.
Don't know why you helped me out of my Scorpio shell, Jazz.

I've long loved the likes of M. Davis and B. Holiday
as well as some of those fusionists who've helped to sell jazz.

Jazz, you always preferred alt-rock over other genres.
I'm glad you still accepted me – this nerd for modal jazz.

Nowadays, when someone asks me my fave form of music,
I smile in my sunnies, pause for effect…and then yell, 'Jazz!'

I note there's more than one alternative way to spell 'Jazz'.
I hope that you're well and like the sound of this ghazal, Jazz.

Wind Chimes

    wind

        chimes out

            forgotten names

     plays

              jazz drums

  on my tympanic

       membranes

           i find myself

lost

       irretrievably so

            surrendering

   once more

     to the ~~sweet~~ pseudo

random whorls

            of this strange

    atmosphere

Pre-Reformation Tea Party

Bendigo, Dja Dja Wurrung Country, late 2000s

This backyard party might as well be a '90s party,
I think to myself as I listen to The Tea Party.

Someone hands me a compact disc containing all six tracks
on the '90s EP *Alhambra* by The Tea Party.

The name of this Ontarian band keeps making me think
of protestors who threw tea at the Boston Tea Party.

I've never done drugs but now I smell weed in the warm air.
From my spot, I cannot make out the (un)guilty party.

I still feel like a member of the Australian Greens
whose voice means little to the parliamentary party.

I wish Jeff would get this prog rock band back together now,
I think out soft-loud as I listen to The Tea Party.

One Halloween

I jumped into a jumpsuit
and pinned on a homemade name tag
that read 'VENKMAN'
in red font.

I rocked up at a Halloween party
to the sound of 'Monster Mash' –
not the Ghostbusters theme –
and proceeded to pull off

a poor Venkman impression,
complete with warm expression.

I left my plastic proton pack
at the front door,
feeling no need to pretend
to bust ghosts on Halloween.

I just got a green drink
and mingled with monsters.

Dolphins

I was half-listening to some CD
on my Discman during year 11
English class
when one of my two genuine classmates
slid a CD out of his wallet
and said I should give it a spin.
I asked him what it was called.
He said *The Distance to Here*
by +LIVE+.
I asked him which tracks were good.
He said they all were.
After pressing that disc in & pressing play,
I intently listened to the music & lyrics
during each English class,
learning language on multiple levels.
While I agreed with my mate's review,
I found myself coming back to one track
repeatedly –
'The Dolphin's Cry'.
Its slow verses & bridge
created a liquid atmosphere –
formed a saltwater lake of sound
from which the chorus emerged like the cry of dolphins.

                                                               Ten
                                                               years
                                                               later

I was half-listening to the fade-out
of Regina Spektor's 'Laughing With'
on Triple J
during a stats study sess
when one of my two fave presenters
suggested listeners listen
to Spektor's new album
Far.
I refrained from calling in
to ask her which tracks were good.
After opening a media player & pressing play,
I intently listened to the music & lyrics
during the rest of my stats degree,
learning language on multiple levels
& maths on multiple planes.
While I enjoyed the whole album,
I found myself coming back to one track
repeatedly –
'Folding Chair'.
Its bubbly verses, bridge & chorus
created a liquid atmosphere –
formed a saltwater lake of sound
from which Spektor's dolphinesque cries emerged.

(Mis)pronunciation

My new friend from Germany
asks me in perfect English
if I know any German.

'*Einfach*,'
I mispronounce
in Aussie English.

'*Wunderbar!*' she replies,
surprised.

After   a pause,
I proceeding to share
an oddly vivid memory
from those formative years
before I'd become
a biostatistician…

I
was an
18-year-old
seated in a ~~silent~~
secondary school library
listening to Powderfinger's Oz
number 1 album *Odyssey Number 5*
on CD while studying year 12 mathematics.

A classmate from my chemistry
class was seated   across from me
studying German.

Red pen in hand,
she reached across
to my page full of complex
planes & imaginary
numbers

to scrawl a single word
in the margin:
Einfach.

Pressing pause on my Discman,
I peered at her quizzically.

'It means easy,'
she whispered
with a quokka grin.

'That maths is so easy
compared to this language
I'm studying.'

'I think I agree,'
I said sincerely
before something like silence
resumed…

My mouth & eyes grin
at this long-forgotten recollection
as I walk
with my new friend from Germany.

In response, she mirrors
my Duchenne grin
& declares in perfect Denglish
'Well, for me, German's *einfach.*'

(H)ear

        Each voice
    is unique. Each voice belongs.
   Each voice belongs to one individual
  member of a diverse choir of voices rising up
 above the ambience. Each voice is the culmination
of air passing from lungs to larynx, strumming vocal
cords & arriving at the tongue as…sound. Each voice is
a combination of sounds moulded by mouth muscles…
Each voice rides the highs and the lows of sound waves
at varying volumes and pitches, swiftly making its way
through the atmosphere. Each voice soon reaches the
ear. Each voice travels thru the auditory canal then
beats out its groove on the eardrum. Each voice
has a butterfly effect on the complex anatomy
of the ear, making bones fluids membranes
and hairs move like machine parts. Each
voice ends up electric. Each voice may
take one or more forms & enter our
brains via varied senses, from au
ral to tactile to visual. Each
voice is silent right up
to the moment it's
heard.

She Who Rocks

Adelaide, Kaurna Country, 19 June 2015

I roll up to a gig at The Gov called She Who Rocks
with a South Australian friend from uni – she too rocks.

We're here to hear homegrown bands helmed by Sarah & Suze –
'90s-era rockers who're as solid as two rocks.

We hear The Superjesus start with(out) 'Gravity'.
My mind floats between Neptune & Earth, between blue rocks.

We rush forward as Baby Animals start their set –
their hyperenergetic opener 'Rush You' rocks.

We can't believe both bands were dropped from Day on the Green
to leave a line-up that could've been called He Who Rocks.

(Broken) hearts sing along to Baby Animals' 'One Word'.
Soon Suze & Sarah share a mic – water flows through rocks.

When the last encore ends and I say bye to my friend,
I take the tram home and ponder one word – not two – rocks.

(Im)mortal Coils

I.

At 21,
I flew to Florence
and promenaded past
Romanesque & Gothic buildings,
stopping every second moment
to snap some shots.
I lagged behind my tour group
and got lost
amidst the architecture.
In an uncertain state, I stopped
outside a house dedicated to Dante
to sit
and listen to Lacuna Coil
echo their melodic metal
through corded
earphones.

II.

At 39,
I stayed in Strathfieldsaye
and pondered the past.
I listened to Baroque songs online,
stopping every second moment
to hear out advertisements.
I lagged behind music trends
and got lost
amidst classical recordings.
In a certain state, I stopped
on *Caccini: Sacred & Secular Songs*
and sat
to listen to Francesca Caccini
echo her robust 'Romanesca'
through cordless
earphones.

Uamh Bhin, or The Melodious Cave

after Felix Mendelssohn's The Hebrides Overture (Fingal's Cave) *[1833]*

We're afloat on the Sea of the Hebrides. We're surrounded by the sort of seawater that glistens turquoise 'gainst cerulean skies. We listen to seawater's splash & engine's vroom – sounds that sustain a tension as taut as the strings of well-strung violas & cellos bowed to imperfection. We listen to our tour guide's woodwind voice – the bold buzzing of a bassoon blown to imperfection. Soon enough, we're acutely aware of that ebb & flow of the Sea of the Hebrides. It's as though we're now listening to the crescendo & diminuendo of violins scoring the last few nautical miles of our pleasurable pilgrimage from the Isle of Mull to Staffa – a basalt island that has been growing & growing in our respective viewpoints, gradually revealing its key coastal features, gradually revealing its sea cave. The much-discussed and -snapped drama of the scene suddenly becomes real to us, suddenly manufactures a masterful melody that soars over rough seawater to completely capture our post-information-age attention. We actively listen. We hear the lapping & crashing of seawater on basalt – that timeless timpani rhythm. Soon enough, our soles touch basalt & carry us towards the barely lit recesses of a natural cathedral with supernatural acoustics. We find ourselves awed reverent revenant resonant, our varied voices becoming the bold buzzing of brass instruments: trumpets & horns. Someone voices their philosophy about each human being an island with a sea cave amidst an island chain. Someone else voices their philosophy about each human being the saltwater that fills a sea cave amidst an island chain. Someone else voices their philosophy about each human being dying. Our varied voices echo echo echo echo off the rough basalt columns. These sounds resonate. These sounds stay with us when our bodies reluctantly return to that moored pontoon boat for the rest of our return voyage. As the engine vrooms, our brass-cum-woodwind spirits are still moved by that cavernous rhythm… moved to follow it up up up up above the rough seawater, to rise up & harmonise with strings in tideless heavens.

Numerology

While tuning in
to ABC Classic 2
on a wintry afternoon,
I appreciate successive recordings
of Kats-Chernin's *Wild Swans Suite No. 2*
+ Chopin's *Piano Sonata No. 2*.
Switching across
to Double J,
I pay attention to the studio version
of Radiohead's '2 + 2 = 5'.
I'm left wondering whether these radio stations
or the Universe
are trying to say something more significant
or not.
Perhaps I'm reaching too far for (il)logical patterns
in this bittersweet chaos.

Two Branches

after Regina Spektor's song 'Blue Lips' from her album Far *(Sire, 2009) as well as Brendan T. Sharkey's cover art for this album*

Regina Spektor
singing about our speck
               of blue
    in the depths of space
makes me contemplate
the complex

formulas & figures
of acoustics
as well as optics –
the branch of physics
               that illuminates
our limited understanding
of how on Earth light
radiates, propagates
& crafts colours
for open eyes.

Regina Spektor
playing her blue piano
               solo
in some room in New York
makes me contemplate
the complex

formulas & figures
of optics
as well as acoustics –
the branch of physics
> that amplifies

our slender understanding
of how on Earth sound
vibrates, propagates
& makes music
for inner ears.

Regina Spektor
performing 'Blue Lips'
stills my tongue & my mind,
silences me into studying
> divine blueprints

for all sights and sounds
in the Universe.

Music Critics Tread a Fine Line

        noteworthy noteworthy not worthy not worthy
        noteworthy noteworthy not worthy not worthy

```
        n                                               n
        o                                               o
        t                                               t
        e
        w                                               w
        o                                               o
        r                                               r
        t                                               t
        h                                               h
        y                                               y
 noteworthy  note                              not worthy   not
worthy  noteworthy                             worthy  not worthy
 noteworthy  note                              not worthy   not
     worthy                                         worthy
```

Traversing the Soundscapes

after the prog rock song 'Luminol' from Steven Wilson's album The Raven that Refused to Sing and Other Stories *(Kscope, 2013)*

I went there
on a motionless journey
of approximately 12 minutes' duration –
about one-and-a-half times longer
than the time it's supposed to take
for the Sun's photons

to reach & reflect off
the ~~friendly~~ faces
of our Earth & Moon

throughout that whole period,
I was a body oscillating
through transient states
of sentiment

going through phases
of regression & progression
reminiscent of time
-lapsed footage of tidal waters
ebbing & flowing

it was a scenic trip
with gothic scenery
and sci-fi mechanics

the ambience
was multidimensional
and lush,
the production value –
high

I was somehow travelling
at varied high speeds through space
-time

I was hurtling into/along/beyond
the multifaceted mathematics of music

my heart beat
out of time with that 4/4 signature

I trembled & spaced out
at the treble & bass clefs

I   at
  quivered   quavers

I took note
of emotive
soundscapes
featuring
funky bass/syncopated beats/atmospheric keys/sprawling guitars/
clean vocals

if I had a hat on,
I would've thrown it in the air
to Alan Parsons

for I could've been listening
to Pink Floyd regress & progress
from & to *The Dark Side*
of the Moon

I could've sworn

I discerned occasional outbursts

                                       of jazz flute & sax

as well as something else entirely –
was that the mellotron
or some other sampler?

it was some soundtrack(!)
for a supernatural story

I felt
as though I were riding a roller coaster
                    travelling
at the speed of sound

I was torn apart by riffs & rhythms
soothed by harmonies & melodies
enthralled by verses & vocalising
about a bad busker & the hereafter

if there was a chorus,

     I completely missed it

if there was no chorus,

     I didn't miss it at all

towards the end
of my sonic sojourn,
I found myself
sweetly yet soundly
beat

into substitution
& hopelessly hopeful
that a rave of Australian ravens
would soon swoop in to spirit

me away
to my lounge chair
& cold cup of hot chocolate

Golden Satellite

a golden shovel after Omar Musa's woodcut print Leopard Made of Midnight Clouds *(2019)*

Today I feel so tired,
though the thing(s) I'm tired of
elude(s) me. Perhaps I'm tired of the
               selective reporting on the news
or maybe I'm tired of not being (re)tired

or maybe I'm tired of the incessant sounds of
traffic streaming past my place and along the

highway. Is it that superhighway – the net –
that I'm tired
of?
Is it my comorbid anxiety
that I'm tired
of?
I cannot help but harbour regret

over having spent so
much time flying solo. I
keep thinking of that time I fell

in a hole & rolled my ankle. I strive to be asleep
right throughout the night and
struggle to recall all I've dreamed.

I feel good when I read books, view art or listen to i
-Tunes or similar. I wonder: if I was
in fact a track about a
big cat, would I be RR's 'Fast as a Leopard',
YYY's 'Gold Lion' or RHCP's 'Slow Cheetah'? I once made

the major mistake of
trying to learn trumpet: I stayed up past midnight
each night trying but, unlike Flea, failed. Mist still clouds

my views of vistas and
keeps me in my place – this space where the
semi-darkness somehow shines bright.

Whenever I peer through gumtrees at the Moon,
I wonder how & why that satellite has shone
on us for so long, how & why it shines through
Earth's atmosphere and into the heart of me.

Blue Thought

I
Am
Afraid
That I shan't
Be able to think
In a straight line for
Yet another 24-hour cycle.
My old train of blue
Thought is still
Moving in a
Jagged
Line.
I
Am
Afraid
That I shall
Be going down
To my dark vault of
Deeply painful memories.
History will support
Bluest thoughts
And wreck
Another
Day.

I
Am
Afraid
That I shall
Soon turn into
A worthless failure
Who languishes in misery
Irritation vacillation
And frustration.
It'll just be
Another
Day.
I
Am
Afraid
That I shall
Liken myself to
A sea anemone on
A deep, dark ocean floor.
I'm eternally stuck
In the one spot
Facing just
Another
Day.

I
Am
Afraid
That I shall
Be quite sleepy
Throughout the day.
My mum's range of brain
Food will do what it
Can to catapult
Me through
Another
Day.
I
Am
Afraid
That I shall
Soon perspire
And shake all over
As I fret about trivialities.
A racing heart will
Thump out the
Passage of
Another
Day.

I
Am
Afraid
That I shall
Be alone with
These jagged, blue
Thoughts for far too long.
What a pitiful way
To realise that
I've wasted
Another
Day.
I
Am
Afraid
That all the
Behemoths in
My vault will arise
When I go to bed tonight.
Another long night
Will bleed into
The blue of
Another
Day.

I
Am
Afraid
That I shall
Be afraid. I'm
Afraid that I shall
Ache. I am afraid that I
Can't be the only
Pained soul to
Detest each
Passing
Day.
I
Am
Afraid
That many
People struggle
With mental illness.
We need others to

I
N
T
E
R
R
U
P
T

Our trains of blue
Thought and

R
  E
    D
      I
        R
          E
            C
              T

                    U
                      S

                          T
                            O

                                    BETTER DAYS.

First Dance

after Florence + the Machine's song 'Shake it Out' from the album Ceremonials *(Island, 2011) and the music video by Dawn Shadforth*

every other night is like Halloween
without the upbeat celebrations
without individually wrapped treats
to give or receive

it's difficult for us to breathe
at difficult times –
hearts a racing, hands a shaking
melancholic memories on loop

we hear we ought to try
to catch some breaths + shake it all out
to go against our golden rule
to never dance

we start to dance
as we start to realise
there's no need for masquerade masks
in the pre-dawn darkness
of our convalescence

Applied Neuroscience

*after Benee's song 'Bagels' (Benemusicc Limited, 2023), which was
created in collaboration with Youthline NZ, ASB and neuroscientists*

When
I hear her voice
    hum & speak
over the silkiest of beats,
my unfocussed mind flows
into a kind of meditative state
and focusses on fondest memories
of your memorable face.

    When
    I hear her voice
        hum & speak
    over the silkiest of beats,
    I'm reminded of those two
    wonderful weeks spent with you
    savouring salmon bagels on the coast
    of Awabakal Country.

        When
        I hear her voice
            hum & speak
        over the silkiest of beats,
        those immersive feelings
        of anxiousness & loneliness
        swirl so sweetly away
        down the drain.

Sheepwash Creek Ginko[1]

Strathfieldsaye, Dja Dja Wurrung Country

i.

creekside –
river red gums
creak

ii.

perched
on a river red gum branch –
an Aussie wood duck
goes *gnaarrk…*

iii.

amidst birdsongs –
Eastern banjo frogs
resonate

iv.

I walk along this creek –
all fellow walkers
say hi

---

[1] Ginko is the Japanese term for a haiku walk, which involves going on a walk to find inspiration for haiku writing.

Well-being

i.

simply sitting
at home with Covid
lapdogs
on pyjamaed laps,
making art
while half-listening
to recordings recur

ii.

simply strolling
outside with Covid
lapdogs,
cutting laps
round walking tracks

iii.

simply meeting
social contacts
at al fresco cafés
to fortify
biochemistry

iv.

simply viewing that photo
of my mother
 standing
at the head of the picnic table
in her crimson coat

v.

somehow sitting
safely in a crowd
on the local limestone
of Epidaurus Theatre,
intently listening
to live vocals
reverberate

vi.

soundly   sleeping

Closer

Adelaide, Kaurna Country, 14 November 2019

It was the closing session on the dying day of the oncology conference. I'd sat down near the front of the crowded auditorium. Wiping the remnants of afternoon tea from my Movember mo, I tuned into the armchair convo between Adam Spencer and his interviewee: Kirk Pengilly. Clad in their smart casual clothes, the star pair proceeded to shift the proceedings from scientific studies to stories & songs. I listened as Kirk opened up about the lows & highs of his forty-odd years as a vocal & multi-instrumental member of influential Aussie rock band INXS. I listened as Kirk opened up about his past bandmate & my namesake, Michael – a man who, much like me, was a shy kid yet, much unlike me, became a global rock star. I listened as Kirk opened up about a part of himself: his sudden diagnosis of life-threatening prostate cancer & the subsequent removal of his prostate via radical prostatectomy. I listened as Kirk shared further life stories, including anecdotes about his supportive wife: pro surfer Layne Beachley. I felt Kirk spoke as both a survivor of cancer & a supporter of men's health across many dimensions, from physical to emotional. I felt that, if I'd looked around, I'd have seen a crowd of conference delegates fully attuned to the conversation. As I pondered Movember with ears wide open, Kirk Pengilly proceeded to close the proceedings with his acoustic set of INXS staples. He closed on the same song I recalled resounding through St Andrew's Cathedral in late spring '97 – back when Kirk & his bandmates helped a grieving brother carry Michael's casket into dark daylight.

Sliding and Rising

after the painting An Afternoon Adrift *(acrylic paint on canvas, 2019) by Andrew Bennett*

You're letting those competing demands slide for five hours; you've clocked off for an overdue afternoon of self-care.

You're seated on the floor in the sliding doorway again, as if unsure whether to slide in or slip out into the lukewarm light of day.

You're reading one of Maya Angelou's autobiographies again, all the while wishing you wouldn't have to soon slide your bookmark back in.

You're sliding thong-clad feet up that sliding door again, your long legs rising up in ripped denim, one hand holding a mug half full of hibiscus tea.

You're hearing those hooks within that Goo Goo Dolls song 'Slide' again, this time through beige buds hidden neath golden tresses that fade away in shadows.

You're sliding into a parallel universe again, your other, more stressful lives still unspooling like those lives led by the protagonist Paltrow played in *Sliding Doors*.

You're romanticising your recurring dream
of swiftly sliding
down the
science
centre's
vertical
slide again
& again & again
ahead of heading home to fall asleep alone.

You're sliding into a fresh daydream of gently rising through the troposphere in your tiny house, your mind warming to this revelation of a calmer journey   to   Oz.

Stress-soothing Songs

I've been known to get light
-hearted grief
for ~~still~~ listening

to turn-of-the-millennium All Saints
while recommending the aural experience.
I wanna go

on the record to say I don't care.
When I wanna let down
my greying black hair
& relax
away
life's incessant stress,
precious few tunes

could match the beats & sweet tones
of turn-of-the-millennium All Saints
on their twin tracks
'Black Coffee' & 'Pure Shores'.

Whenever these All Saints songs
arise from my music archives
in one audio format
or another,
I go

to that place.
I find myself
savouring sugary black coffee
with someone special

on the balcony of a beach house
somewhere
amidst these isolated islands
of Oceania.

Trajectory

My black sedan
moves me
along a long highway

to purgatory at a steady
100 kilometres
per hour.

I zoom through a pastoral landscape
lit by the swiftly shifting light
of day – this summer solstice.

Glancing sidelong,
I tune in to the sight
of a soft saffron sunset

and sense serenity
descending.

The silhouettes of gumtrees
form Australian gothic patterns
of fractals amidst calm chaos

calling to mind the loveless ghost
       of my ex-lover
clad all in black.

Through trunks & branches,
the still waters of a lake
reflect fading light

and call to mind the loving spirit
        of my dear mother
clad all in white.

   The hum

of my black sedan
moving
along a long highway

helps make me meditative.

I pull over for a power nap
& dream I'm already home.

Fluidal

Strathdale, Dja Dja Wurrung Country, December 2021

Since the start of the decade,
I've rediscovered
the vibrations of   a t o m s
the arrow of time
the manifestations of chaos theory
the manifestos of Dadaists.

Since the start of the decade,
I've sat with
my perceptions
    self-deceptions
        apprehensions
           morbidity
              mortality
                & morality.

Since the start of the decade,
I've said my goodbyes
to my workmates
   my dying mother
& my departing partner.

Since the start of the decade,
I've been drinking
from a bottomless cup
of up
            -HEAV-
                          al.

Since the start of the decade,
I've discovered
the simple pleasure
of lapping local lakes
with my lapdog
while noticing
endemic birds

                              call.

Khronos

I recall walking
in my work shoes
through the waiting room
each workday.

I recall all the patients
sitting & waiting
alone
or with a number
of others
to see oncology staff.

I recall thinking
each one of them
could've been anyone
waiting
to see anyone:

>a general practitioner
>a public servant
>railway staff
>airline staff
>performers
>athletes
>anyone
>at all.

I recall hearing
the celebration bell
ring in the distance
for someone
other than
these patients.

I recall recalling
all the repetition
in the chorus
of Sheryl Crow's
'Make it Go Away
(Radiation Song)'.

I recall thinking
These patient
cancer patients
are people
like Mum.

I recall seeing,
hearing and
6th sensing
a familiar
person
seated
right
there.

I remember
Mum.

I Recall When the Kind ICU Staff Kept Calm

                        I recall
when the kind ICU staff kept calm
    -ly telling us that my dear mother
had become critically unstable,
    that her young heart now pumped
faintly, that her once elevated BP
    kept on falling & falling & falling
away, that her kidneys & her liver
    had been starved of blood & gone
into shock, that meds & machines
    had taken over from all of her vital
organs, that she was comfortable
    with all those tubes in the hospital
bed, that each of us should ready
    ourselves to hear the worst possible
news.
    When the kind ICU staff kept calm
-ly saying these mournful things,
    I utterly lost the power of speech
– the ability to cry my lungs out
    as each word cut a fresh wound,
the ability to ask docs & nurses
    the myriad questions ricocheting
round & round & round & round
    my exhausted & scattered mind,
the ability to comfort my family
    with talk of Mum's strong spirit,
the ability to rush to her bedside
    & tell her *You're the best mother.*
There was just one thing I could do:
                        shake.

Intermission

in the hospital chapel
with my siblings –
silence

Part 2

Love Notes

The Warmth of Her Light

i.

her inclined bed
I look past those tubes
into bright eyes

ii.

hospital carpark
dawn light thru gumtrees
on the day Mum passed

iii.

winter burial
setting sun bursts
while her casket
descends

Life Symbol

It's the most endearing
life symbol from Mum's funeral.

It's the most enduring
life symbol from Mum's funeral.

It's the very best present
her antiquarian mother
ever gave her.

It's her life
        -long
cuddly companion.

It's her thread
-bear plushy.

It's her bear
-like
antique toy.

It's an heir
-loom.

It's a
koala.

Mum's Life and Death Song

As I age
towards death,
I'll never forget
the sights
the sounds
the (e)motions
of departing

Mum's
Service of
Thanksgiving.

I walked
as steadily and silently
as possible
with Mum's white casket
past all those familiar faces
and through certain sound waves

that vibrantly shook the winter air
with one of Mum's fave songs –
the soulful
'I Say a Little Prayer'

by the Queen
of Soul
and of Singing
More Generally –
the late, great
mezzo-soprano
Aretha Franklin.

December Remembrances of the Worst Winter

                over
                        &
                under
                      whelmed

       iso   late   d

be   late   d

       be   reave   d

the prick
             ling
                          losses
                of

     free   doms
           opt   im
                       ism
     cal   end   ar

                       en   tries

                time

     ful   fil
                      ment

        peace   of   mind

conne   X   ions

        to places

              to animals

    to people

the pier

    cing

        loss

  of my dear

      young

          mother

at the   I   C   U

        on the 6th day

          of winter

2 0 2 0

the bitterly cold

  absence

    of her

  presence

    the radiantly warm
                thoughts
                      of her
                      thoughtfulness

                                            open shutters
                                shed light on her table
                                      of photographs

Twenty-Six Things I Remember about My Mother

1. Her aptitude for antiquities
2. Her briskly read books
3. Her celebrated celebrations
4. Her demure dresses
5. Her everyday endurance
6. Her fantastic food
7. Her genuine generosity
8. Her heart-warming heart
9. Her in-demand intuition
10. Her jolly jokes
11. Her knowledge of knickknacks
12. Her lively loquaciousness
13. Her Motown music
14. Her no-nonsense nature
15. Her optimal originality
16. Her philosophical philosophy
17. Her quixotic questions
18. Her resilient relationship
19. Her sublime selflessness
20. Her tireless truthfulness
21. Her unknown undertakings
22. Her virtuous volunteerism
23. Her way with wrought words
24. Her X-marked X-rays
25. Her yearned-for yesterdays
26. Her zigzag sign of the zodiac

Gratitunes

Thank you, dear mother,
for getting me into soul,
most notably
the music of
Four Tops,
The Supremes
& Aretha Franklin.

Thank you, dear sister,
for getting me into pop rock,
most notably
the music of
Paramore,
Lana Del Rey
& My Chemical Romance.

Thank you, dear brother,
for getting me into ska,
most notably
the music of
Area-7,
No Doubt
& Mighty Mighty Bosstones.

Thank you, dear father,
for getting me
to occasionally
take
out
my headphones
& tune in to the ambience.

Quintet

after a framed family photograph taken in 2006

My fave number is five – that prime number of people from my nuclear family. The five of us are frozen in poses here in the studio for our first & only family portrait. Our clothes are colour-coordinated courtesy of a costume designer… courtesy of my mother. Mum has remained diamond-willed about my younger sister and I wearing these similar shirts she'd seen us sport separately. My clothes now mirror those of my younger sister – her shirt shows Emily the Strange, mine that Franz Ferdinand band logo. The black-and-red stripes of our matching shirts match my black hair and my sister's red hair. The black-and-red stripes of our matching shirts ain't only alt & emo – they're the partial tartan of our part-Scottish lineage. The black-and-red stripes of our matching shirts are horizontal or vertical, depending on your viewpoint. The red in the black-and-red stripes of our matching shirts matches our shared lifeblood. The black in the black-and-red stripes of our matching shirts matches these outfits around us: our elder brother's black V-neck jumper worn while playing bass in a local ska outfit; our father's black leather jacket worn while vending antiques at certain Sunday markets around rural Vic; our mother's black overcoat worn while stocking up on stock at shops, stalls, auctions & elsewhere… It appears I'm still seated here beside my sister. Our brother is behind us, our father's too far, our mother's leaning on my left shoulder. I can still feel Mum right here. I can still feel Mum within the frame of this photo & the frame of my first home. I can still feel my mother all these years after we laid her body to rest in the loud wake of bagpipes.

Familial

It's a song that's always been a real powerhouse. I managed to combine that gospel thing (mentioned earlier) with the power chords, with the big guitars…it just gives it that whole…cinematic flavour.
Jimmy Barnes on his song 'When Your Love is Gone', Days Like These with Diesel, *2022*

It's just another lazy Saturday in August. I'm sat at my laptop watching & listening to the 7th episode in the 2022 series *Days Like These with Diesel* – an episode where Barnesy sits to sing at Sydney Opera House in August 2007. Too soon, the bar has moved across to the final 7 minutes of this generous 53-minute episode. As Barnesy's brother-in-law, Diesel, declares *Last song…'When Your Love is Gone'*, I hear that long-forgotten melody and those powerful words sung to such perfect imperfection by a voice that howls soulfully in harmony with loved ones… Suddenly, it's some other day back in 1991. I'm sat in a station wagon watching windows & listening to Barnesy's recording of 'When Your Love is Gone' from one of my folks' fave cassettes – *Two Fires*. That thirty-something man is singing with his kids, The Tin Lids. I'm only 7; my nearby brother is 9. We have no sister yet. My thirty-something father is driving; my thirty-something mother is beside him. We're en route from Bendigo to a holiday destination – most likely Ballarat or Adelaide, perhaps even the Gold Coast, no doubt someplace with tourist attractions for kids. Turning from the passing scenery, I speak happily with my young family whilst Barnesy sings harmoniously with his. Being so young, I selectively savour the snacks from the road trip but not the sounds of the road trip. Too soon, the outro fades like consciousness… Suddenly, I'm back in the modern day watching orange credits flash by and listening to Diesel's theme tune, 'Days Like These'. I'm back in this time when my brother & I have a baby sister as well as a father who's a widower – one of two fires blown apart.

Over the Rainbow

We state
the sweet simple things
you yearned to do
on your ICU deathbed:

to return home
& keep cooking meals
for others;

      to go out
in your new second-hand car
& buy bargain-priced antiques
at op shops.

As we speak about you,
your song comes on
the car radio: 'Over the Rainbow'
by your namesake.

Judy's angelic vocals
coupled with the   soaring
instrumental arrangement
strike major chords
and render us
speechless.

I recall how you adored
this sweet simple song
we haven't heard
in so   long,
how the funeral
director mistakenly played
that cover version you abhorred

at your burial.

During this rare moment
with my baby sister,
I look her in the face –

tears falling
from familiar eyes
reflect mine
as we draw ever closer
to our final destination.

Here I am –
an off-duty statistician –
wholeheartedly believing
in the beautiful spirituality
of synchronicity.

Lily

after 'The Raven that Refused to Sing' from Steven Wilson's album The Raven that Refused to Sing and Other Stories *(Kscope, 2013)*

The first song
that made me cry
on first listen, I mean
properly cry –

weep out my pent-up store of lacrimal secretions
while home alone in my bare bedroom –
was a three-note song

based on Poe's poem 'The Raven',
namely Steven Wilson's
'The Raven that Refused to Sing'.

The haunting
vocals piano guitars drums wind strings
overcame me.

Most notably,
Steven's straightforward chorus
about someone losing someone
named not Lenore but Lily
called to mind someone
so important in my life,
someone

young at heart who had recently passed
away from my maternal grandpa:
my maternal grandma,   Lily.

Grandpa's Acoustic Guitar

i.

In his younger years, my maternal grandfather was a country singer & guitarist with a booming voice & nimble fingers. He sounded like Slim Dusty. Grandpa played sets across unspoilt lands, from the smallest towns to the biggest cities. My late mother once told me Grandpa performed for Queen Elizabeth II at an outdoor concert in '54 – the year after she was born. I've always believed that anecdote unconditionally as I never knew Mum to tell furphies.

ii.

My elder brother followed in Grandpa's boot prints, becoming the youngest guitarist in the family. He grew into a great guitarist – a muso with many CDs & MP3s to his name. He would've sounded like Grandpa & Slim Dusty if all his guitars were acoustic rather than electric, if his genres were country & folk rather than punk & ska.

iii.

My baby sister followed in Grandpa's boot prints, becoming the youngest vocalist in the family. She grew into a superb singer – a songbird with many musical theatre credits to her name. She would've sounded like Kasey Chambers if her vocals had a certain country twang, if she sang country & folk songs rather than West End & Broadway numbers.

iv.

My maternal grandparents had a happy home amidst the ironbarks. Grandma looked like Mrs Bucket from *Keeping Up Appearances*, Grandpa like John Hammond from *Jurassic Park*. They were infinitely kinder & humbler than their on-screen lookalikes. Their hearts were warm yet light – younger than their older years. One bleak morning, the love of Grandpa's life passed on amidst a hospitalisation. Grandpa moved into a nursing home on the same street as their old home, leaving all his acoustic guitars behind. By that point, Grandpa hadn't performed or recorded in several decades. His albums of country & folk songs had never been on CDs or MP3s, let alone streaming services. They'd only ever been on records & cassettes – old storage devices that'd wound up in storage… alongside his acoustic guitars.

v.

One day, us (grand)sons & (grand)daughters thought we'd surprise Grandpa by getting his eldest acoustic guitar cleaned & restrung. We hand-delivered that old chordophone to Grandpa's room at the nursing home. Grandpa accepted his possession with gratitude and a grin. He then handed it back to us, without so much as one strum with fingers or plectrum. He asked us to place that old chordophone in the corner of his austere room, within its accompanying stand. When we asked Grandpa to play us a song, he politely declined. It took us too long to realise that Grandpa's knuckles had become so inflamed – so arthritic – he could no longer play guitar.

vi.

Grandpa's osteoarthritis coexisted with comorbidities. One of them was cancer. With time, the metastatic melanoma atop Grandpa's head stopped responding to radiation therapy and started to sap his life force. My family and I started visiting him more often. I found myself thinking: *I'd trade all my healthy knuckles to hear that dear old man play 'Waltzing Matilda' one last time.* It would've been something special. It would've been an older performer's belated encore for the most intimate of audiences. One balmy morning, Grandpa was transferred from his nursing home to the local hospice. Over the weeks that followed, I found myself listening to that duet by Slim Dusty and Kasey Chambers – 'Matilda No More' – on loop. One bleak morning, I found Grandpa open-mouthed & motionless in his hospice room, uncharacteristically quiet. The quiet lingered for a moment before shattering & shattering & shattering. Over the weeks that followed, I found myself listening to Emily Wurramara's 'Black Smoke' on loop.

vii.

The day Grandpa passed on, my baby sister somehow still took to the stage as Morticia in a local musical production of *The Addams Family*. She somehow sang her big number – '(Death is) Just Around the Corner' – to perfection. It was a bittersweet tribute to Grandpa. I've never been prouder of anyone, not in all my life. Some days later, I tried to read out my elegiac poem for Grandpa at his burial beneath the gumtrees. Much unlike the rehearsals at home, my body & voice shook nonstop throughout the poetry reading. I dropped my unfolded piece of paper six feet.

viii.

It's been years since my maternal grandparents & mother passed on. It's been seven decades since Grandpa performed music for a young monarch. Grandpa's eldest acoustic guitar is now something else: an heirloom on a rack in the beating heart of my elder brother's home. It's perfectly still there in the guitar rack. It's a lone acoustic guitar amidst electric guitars, every one of its strings still un-strummed.

Elvis

Bendigo Art Gallery, May 2022

gallery entrance –
a black-and-white headshot
framed in gold

round platform –
Elvis' white MG painted
lipstick-red

technicolour clips
from Elvis movies
& concerts on loop

stage full of mannequins
dressed
in the King's colourful jumpsuits

lone display case
against an off-white wall –
his black guitar

amidst treasures –
gold-plated phone
from Elvis' bedside

heart of the gallery –
a black-and-white tux
with a white dress

Temporelle[1]

Those steady ticks
are heartbeats transcending
incessant chaos,
bringing future moments

composed of slowly fading memories
d'heures chéries avec tois[2]
on sun-kissed
days.

If you were still in your elements here
I'd whisper sweet somethings in both your ears

        in the hope we'd soon start
        to slow dance to the music of our breaths.

I'd then decide you're even more mesmerising
than Julia Stone slow dancing
while breathing out verses in fluent *Française.*[3]

I can't help wondering:
when did it dawn on me that you're the one?
Perhaps when I gave you more attention

after you gave me two hands
amidst the dunes of time's sands.

The trickle
        of water led to ripples then a wave
                that swept up the two of us to lofty heights.

I reread memoirs whose pages rustle
    – like old calendars –
through months when you're well

through months when you're so alive
through months when I'm illumined by your *lumière*[4]
through months when I'm beside myself
while your life
    force
fades.

Whenever I'm alone out there in space
-time,
the sound of atmospheric air
echoes the name of one who lost her life
young.

Cet amour[5]
has long outlasted
cancers.

---

1. *Temporelle* – Temporal
2. *d'heures chéries avec tois* – cherished hours with you
3. *Française* – French
4. *lumière* – light
5. *Cet amour* – This love

Armchair Travelling in January 2021

That Covid summer, I spent my holidays
armchair travelling on every chair in the house
whilst listening to travel
-themed tracks
on loop.
At one point, I found myself
wondering if it's coincidental
that the most successful singles in Angus & Julia Stones'
back catalogue are tracks about travel:
'Chateau'
& 'Big Jet Plane'.
Whilst wondering,
I found myself raiding the printer
and proceeding to fold & fly paper aeroplanes
to the sounds of Angus & Julia Stone
performing a less successful
single: 'Paper Aeroplane'.

A Pastoral for Nate & Damien

Shire of Hepburn, Dja Dja Wurrung Country, 27 November 2021

Red dust rises with my spirits
as I pull into the parking lot
and walk in the footprints
of guests in garden attire.

Reaching paddock-fringed gardens,
I stand amongst familiar faces
of long-lost mates
and feel my grin grow.

I meet my mate's husband-to-be
for the very first time.
I now know this rural bloke –
Damien – is Nate's ideal match.

Soon each groom
walks down a natural aisle
with his sister & his canine
to sounds of sincerest acoustic music.

Their self-penned vows bring
tender laughter & many an *aww*.
Their formal vows bring
them together on legal paper.

As night falls on grazed farmland,
we eat from gourmet food trucks
and raise our matching stubby holders
to Nate's off-the-cuff speech
about obstacles & gratefulness.

Lovecats Triolet

after a Visual Verse *image by Erica Marsland Huynh*

My fave song from my birth year, 1983,
is The Cure's jazz pop track about two loved-up cats.
Though animal imagery may be musty,
my fave song from my birth year, 1983,
portrays people as felines who live to be free.
This heart keeps scatting the same way Robert Smith scats.
My fave song from my birth year, 1983,
is The Cure's jazz pop track about two loved-up cats.

Roxette Triolet

after the movie Super Mario Bros. *(1993)*

My fave part of that *Super Mario Bros.* flick
is Marie Fredriksson singing 'Almost Unreal'.
Though I love making Mario jump into bricks,
my fave part of that *Super Mario Bros.* flick:
a pop rock track about romantic magic tricks.
It pays to stay and listen while credits unreel.
My fave part of that *Super Mario Bros.* flick
is Marie Fredriksson singing 'Almost Unreal'.

Triple J Hottest 100 2022 Votes (In Poetic Order)

Thelma Plum's	'Backseat of My Mind'
Phoebe Bridgers'	'Sidelines'
Gang of Youths'	'goal of the century'
King Stingray's	'Camp Dog'
King Princess & Fousheé's	'Little Bother'
Camp Cope's	'Running with the Hurricane'
Hilltop Hoods & Montaigne's	'A Whole Day's Night'
DMA'S'	'Everybody's Saying Thursday's the Weekend'
The Smith Street Band's	'Everyone is Lying to You for Money'
Florence + the Machine's	'Free'

Trees

Strathfieldsaye, Dja Dja Wurrung Country, 18 September 2023

A new week has dawned
outside this all-but-empty house
in the country
that I've come to call home.

As Monday morning
becomes more of a memory,
I stay seated at my desk
with a sick cavoodle on my lap
and a view of grey kangaroos out the window.

Distance is dissolved
by the livestream on my screen:
though I'm here on Dja Dja Wurrung Country,
I could be there on Bunurong Country
attending my institution's once-in-a-generation
referendum event.

I love how speeches & songs
have challenged all that heartless misinformation
in the lead up to this closing song:
a stripped-back cover
of Cold Chisel's 'Flame Trees'
by Loren Ryan & Paul Grabowski.

I hear the pair
perform so powerfully:
Paul impressively presses piano keys,
     accompanying Loren
as she skilfully strums guitar strings
and sings.

Her strong country voice
is less familiar than the voices
of Barnesy & Blasko.
Her strong Country voice is a necessity.

My heart of hearts swells at the sounds
of Loren singing in the revived language
of her Gomeroi ancestors
on either side of the key change
that comes at the bridge.

Her final words of song
soundtrack a sight in the background –
behind the livestream on my screen –
the sight of those grey kangaroos
hopping past gumtrees
across my neighbour's vast paddock
as though it were 65 thousand years ago.

I reflect on something Loren said
right before singing this last song:
to listen
to your heart
when the question is asked.

My heart says a simple 'Yes'
a million times over.

Seasonal Migration

After flying
over verdant land
from NSW back to Vic,
I found that a flock of swift parrots
        had yet again returned
to the gums & bottlebrushes
out the front of my childhood home.

After flying
over saltwater
from Tassie back to Vic,
those critically endangered parrots
        had proceeded to fill the open air
around Dad's neighbourhood with their song –
melodic chimes redolent of a choir
of handbells.

As I actively listened,
        I recalled the hand
-bell choir mix of Björk's 'Who Is It'
without words.

As I actively listened,
        I yet again hoped
this wouldn't be the swift parrots' last
encore here at my (old) home.

The Plight of the Adélie Penguin

Here at the polar
opposite of the Land of
the Bear, native Adélie penguins
assemble in colonies like Melburnians
clad mostly in monochrome.
The male penguins stretch out
their flippers and call out over
the three distinct states of water
(solid, liquid, and vapour) to their
would-be mates. Each couple mates
for life, seeking out one another every
breeding season: October to February.
The couples locate pockets of dry terrain
so that they may build nests from pebbles. They then go on
amidst perennial icescapes so that maternity & paternity leave from their feeding out at sea
so that females & males may take it in turns incubating their eggs
against the truly glacial Antarctic winds. Upon cracking thru
their shells into the pockets of dry terrain,
chicks eat from their parents' mouths until
they have grown up enough to swim, feed,
and breed. Lately, though, there has been
a change in the glacial winds—a growing
disturbance in a delicate balance. On the
peninsula, temp's have warmed to levels
that are no longer beneficial to the local
penguin colonies. All the solid water has
begun to melt and flood pockets of dry
terrain, drowning and freezing Adélie
penguin eggs and chicks. This circle
of life is buckling and breaking in

     the   O
  growing heat.   unhappy feet!

Non-human Nature

after a Visual Verse *image by Marc Schlossman*

Whenever I take precious time
out from the commitments
of contemporary life
to trace a path through greenery
with my greenish eyes,
I tend to feel as light
as a bare blue bag
gently swaying in spring air
without a single gram
of contents to weigh it
down.
At such times,
I try not to see green
in scientific or symbolic senses.
I try not to see green
on a microscopic level
as some chemical called chlorophyll.
I try not to see green
as a stylised textbook illustration
of green light
reflected & refracted
off & through surfaces.
I try not to see green
as a secondary colour,
as a certain blend
of two primary colours:
the blue of the sky
combined

with the yellow of the sun
to give green.
I try not to see green
as those visual manifestations –
those green or greenish splashes –
of my most recent bout of synaesthesia
which stemmed from certain sounds
with no clear connections to green.
I try not to see green
as the green pigmentation
that colours my own irises
& the irises of others.
I try not to see green
as a complex symbol
capable of symbolising
amongst the most positive & negative
aspects of human nature.
Whenever I take precious time
out from the commitments
of contemporary life
to trace a path through greenery
with my greenish eyes,
I try to simply empty
my blue mind
& see green
for what it's long been:
the serenely viridescent
shades of non-human nature.

(Sym)phonic

As Earth spins me to 40, I grow increasingly sensitive to seasons. I see all these deciduous trees change: green leaves, gold leaves, no leaves, blossoms. Those blossoms fall like all the confetti and snow I've never known (yet may one day). My wardrobe keeps growing more varied, more complementary, more weather-appropriate. I got my first scarf in my 40th winter then wore it every day till spring – my birthseason. I shed every layer when summer sizzled too soon then rugged on up again when autumn finally fell. I couldn't stop penning pieces of prose poetry mentioning pieces of (sym)phonic music. As the climate and I kept changing, I added Vivaldi's 'Four Seasons' & Kats-Chernin's 'Symphonia Eluvium' to my daily playlist alongside Norah Jones' 'How I Weep' & The Verve's 'Bittersweet Symphony'. As the cost of living & dying kept rising, I called radio stations to request The Whitlams' 'Blow Up the Pokies' & Tracy Chapman's 'Talkin' Bout a Revolution'. As coral reefs perished without intervention alongside high proportions of fellow species, I made a new playlist with all available versions of Warumpi Band's 'My Island Home', Joni Mitchell's 'Big Yellow Taxi', Midnight Oil's 'Beds Are Burning' & Melissa Etheridge's 'I Need to Wake Up'. As (un)natural disasters intensified worldwide, I called radio stations to request all songs that'd sampled – to varying degrees – Greta Thunberg's climate speeches. I found myself humming along with melodies, singing with sung lyrics, speaking with spoken words from the discomfort of my bank-owned home. I found myself feeling I'd need to work 9 to 5 till 95 just to make the richest richer. I found myself favouring allusion over illusion for the first time. I felt all my overgrown similes fade to leafless metaphors. I kept reaching for the receding limbs of loved ones and traversing the repurposed places of lost species. I felt lost in (un)natural habitats incinerated by idiotic ideas about what constitutes progress. I felt light enough to rise into the troposphere yet heavy enough to fall back to Earth's surface. I felt something favourable or unfavourable more often than numbness. I felt that my mid-life crisis was essentially existential in nature – barrelled feelings fathomable. I belatedly became someone's definition of a poet trying again & again & again to justify their emergence & establishment & existence. I belatedly became aware of all of Earth's epochs, from Hadean to Anthropocene. I belatedly became a citizen scientist trying to philosophise about time, dabbling in eternalism. I belatedly came to recognise twelve of the infinite number of points about time: time is planetary motion; time is magical realism; time is a flip book of perishing still lifes; time is constantly changing change; time is fuel for our flaming failures; time takes time; time is right on time; time is running right out; time is a metronome that just won't stop moving; time is a set of signatures; time is timeless; time is the tireless co-conductor of our bittersweet symphonies.

Musical Styles

The earbud in her ear
resembles a pearl earring.
She embodies
style
while
listening
to whatever she wants.

the story

written in collaboration with Irina Frolova

i.

it all began *i*n the middle
of February o*n*e Friday on a fatigued
hot husk of an af*t*ernoon
she opened   his po*e*m on her phone
her breath caught in he*r* throat
the rest was history   her s*t*ory
his story   their story   *w*aiting for that
weekend in March   *i*n-person meeting
late into the eve*n*ing   champagne
lips   shared b*e*d   shunned sleep   slipping
into   a *d*ream   morning in mid-Autumn

        ii.

        it all began *i*n the midst
        of St Valenti*n*e's day on a warm wishing
        well   of an af*t*ernoon   he saw
        a headshot of h*e*r on his phone   his eyes
        lingered   on he*r* face as words formed
        3 days later   he sen*t* her that poem &
        held his breath a*w*aiting a reply
        whilst fearing   *i*t might never come
        he hadn't do*n*e something so bold before
        alone   in b*e*d   once again   sliding
        into   a *d*ream   of her in autumnal light

Playlist

I first met her online.
Before long, we'd each decided
to put our distant hearts
on the line.

She sent me one link
to one folk song
by this one artist –
one Johnny Flynn –
every day for over one month…
right up till that one fine night
we first met one another in person.

She sent me these folk songs
by this one artist
whose vocal cords & guitar chords
had been stripped back
to help humans get back
to the heady heart of psychogeography.

She sent me these folk songs
with the regularity
of heartbeats
that echo
evermore,
striking chord
after chord in my
rural & remote soundscapes.

I've been listening intently
& repetitively
to every one of her selected songs.

She's the best
DJ.

My Treasure

i.

Sunday morning –
her eyelashes open
against my cheek

ii.

she drives us through bush
-land –
her playlist plays
Flynn's 'Detectorists'

iii.

we cross fields
lit by autumnal sun –
hands join

iv.

on her blanket by the lake –
sounds of birds,
tastes of lips

v.

we embrace in the air
-port –
my name over the PA

vi.

this near-empty plane
lands –
her message
fills my phone screen

vii.

Sunday morning –
       space
beside me

Two Weeks Together

i.

I return –
her tuxedo cat rests
on my garment bag

ii.

morning sun
through the flame tree –
we relish bagels

iii.

mid-walk, we spot
a kookaburra –
stillness

iv.

we kiss
in the nocturnal house –
sugar gliders

v.

late check-in…
our freshly lit fire
fills the fireplace

vi.

log cabin in the bush –
we hear the *Twin Peaks*
theme

vii.

she points out words
carved on the boardwalk's handrails…
poem on swans

viii.

we stroll hand in hand –
wildflowers grow
over old train tracks

ix.

sixteen red roses –
the first time we say
three short words

x.

her moon boot
she   still   steps
me through Cuban salsa

xi.

we share
a private train compartment –
steam

xii.

we wake amidst treetops
& open blinds –
lorikeets

xiii.

lookout
railing over the estuary –
our lock

xiv.

boarding call –
        she walks me as far
                as the departure gate

Between Strathfieldsaye & Speers Point

Affection persists through the darkest days.
This interstate love radiates
from one thousand kilometres away.

Months have flown by since I first met your gaze
and now synced hearts won't deviate.
Affection persists through the darkest days.

To meet face-to-face, we go out of our ways.
We take turns to negotiate
from one thousand kilometres away.

Since Mum passed away, I've been in this daze
that you've helped to alleviate.
Affection persists through the darkest days.

I scroll up & down as my phone displays
all these words we abbreviate
from one thousand kilometres away.

All your words shine like a sunburst of rays
– welcome warmth to appreciate.
Affection persists through the darkest days
from one thousand kilometres away.

Apple-esque, or You're Like My First Celebrity Crush But Better

Dear,
I think of your perfections
& am reminded
of one

        who

            adores flora & fauna
            abhors certain forms of media

            pens pained lyrics
                lined with love

            prefers solitude
            over company

            reflects
            wavelengths   strikingly

            fractures moulds

            sings out her hot heart
            & made mind
            across a low range

            is oft pissed off
            at this bitter

            -sweet
            spoilt

        world
I think
of your perfections and
am reminded of
Fiona

Enshrined

Great Stupa of Universal Compassion, Dja Dja Wurrung Country

We stroll in step
and hand in hand
through a vast sacred place
where negative space

>   is positive.
> Our progress is soundtracked
> by the drums, bells & trumpets
>   of Tibetan tradition
>   replayed
>   through unseen

speakers.
We are but two of billions
           upon billions
of sentient beings
going about their Friday
in a particular place –
in our case the great
stupa
among gumtrees.

>   The lighting strikes
> me as brighter yet similar
>   to lighting
>   in the sacred heart
>   cathedral

back in town.
I see my sweetheart
savouring liminal spaces
and studying spread-out statues,
each one of us finding

>points of fascination
>amidst divine details.

We find ourselves
selectively spinning prayer wheels
and bathing baby Buddhas
whilst mistakenly mispronouncing
mantras.

>I still can't help but feel
>we're becoming something
>more than two tourists
>in a stupa.

We've found ourselves
on a plane
where the timeless question
of West or East
is as meaningless as our existence.

>We're seeking sanctuary
>from all the scrutiny
>outside
>whilst finding ourselves fading
>into the background

music.
I can't see
a way for us to ascend
from this ground
-ed ground
floor
to the spaces
to the layered atmosphere
of those unknown upper levels.

>I'm now closing two eyes
and scenting intense incense
and seeing
how she manages
to transcend the resonance
of soundtracked silence.

I'm taking a sole moment to confess
to one or more spirits
that my love for the living
is more specific
than it is universal.

Falls
Ku-ring-gai Country, 29 October 2023

As we bushwalk, I reflect on this first-timer's fall
for this woman whose mind & hair shine like waterfalls.

We help each other climb through a gully of boulders,
deeply hoping we won't hear a single boulder fall.

I don't do my best impression of Indiana
Jones as I stumble and – failing to recover – fall.

She does an impressive impression of Marion
Ravenwood; I watch her move nimbly and never fall.

As shadows lengthen, we lose sight of the subtle signs
marking out this perilous route to the waterfall.

Feeling lost, we laugh in fear's face and sing words first sung
by TLC: words warning against chasing waterfalls.

She stops atop a boulder to tear a latched leech off
my shin, even though doing so nearly makes her fall.

Suddenly, we hear that blessed burbling up ahead.
We press on, hand in hand, anxious to watch water fall.

As daylight dims, we see a sacred sight through gumtrees:
the misty, glistening torrents of a waterfall.

Steel City

I'm moseying through Newcastle
Museum
with my partner of eight months.
We're learning
about Newcastle's industrial heritage –
a local history constructed
from the mining of planet-harming coal
and the production of modernising steel.

Not far
from the steelmaking ladle & ingot car,
we suddenly spot
something unexpected, something
incongruous, conspicuous, colourful –
a neon sign
glowing across a curated spectrum
in the darkest corner of Newcastle
Museum.

The sign shows a pinkish couple
dancing
in a red-and-orange room
like my partner & I plan to tonight.
Those tiny dancers dance on
the yellow-and-white word 'SILVERCHAIR',
which stands above
the blue words 'NEON BALLROOM'
as well as four gold stars
that look like they belong in a glowing album review.

As I study the sign, I suddenly realise
a quarter of a century has passed
since those three teens from Silverchair –
amongst the most famous of all Novocastrians –
dropped their third studio album
Neon Ballroom
in the wake of that album's dated lead single

'Anthem for the Year 2000'.

My latent memories	of the lyrics
to this arena rock	song – repetitive words
of youth & rebellion	that still resonate with me –
manage to shock	me
from the past	to the present
from single	to coupled
from hapless	to happy
from high school	to the workplace
from 16	to 39
from one millennium	to another
from 1999	to a time when the cover art for an album from my formative years belongs in a museum.

Philology

There are times
I overhear my dear speak a language
I can't comprehend –
Slavic words
far

removed
from the small number of English
words I know
and the even fewer German & French
words I know.
I wouldn't say it's all Greek
to me –   it's Russian.

This happens
when my Russian-Australian partner
       is skyping her dear mother
who still resides in the heart
of her motherland.

Though the semantics are lost
on me, the sensations are not.
At these times, I welcome

reminders
of the healthy mother-child bond
that held my heart together
till it   frac - tured
under the weight of mortality…
then miraculously healed

reminders
of all the living languages
       and cultures
carried forward by peoples
in the names of parents
       grandparents
       ancestors
and descendants

reminders
of those branching
       Polish branches
amidst my mostly British
family oak tree

reminders
that my partner's name –
Irina –
is of Ancient Greek
Ukrainian & Russian
origin
and literally means 'peace'

reminders	reminders
of rereading	of rereading
an old book	a new piece
of A. Pushkin's poetry	of my partner's poetry
comprising page after page	comprising line after line
of English & Russian words	of English & Russian words
printed side by side	printed side by side

reminders
of the undying fact
that rock-solid foundations of fondness
                are far stronger
than shifting gold sands
& snowdrifts.

Reindeer

the constellation of cracks
on these bathroom tiles
looks like a reindeer

thoughts morph
in the study as I study
patterns of rain, dear

you're on my mind when I go
                   out on the porch
to listen to autumnal rain, dear

my tumble dryer
            tumbles dry
clothes soaked in winter rain, dear

I cry as I lounge
in lounge chairs listening
to Amanda Marshall's 'Let It Rain', dear

I sigh as I cook
in the kitchen listening
to Prince's 'Purple Rain', dear

as I lock
the back & front doors,
I hear Enya's 'Echoes in Rain', dear

in the bathroom, I brush floss gargle
for the full duration
of 'November Rain', dear

in bed, I imagine
December skies filled
with flakes of frozen rain, dear

as sleep slowly comes, I ache
for the purest snow
dream
of reindeer after reindeer

Somewhere on Awabakal Country

You show me this place

        where lush lands embrace salt waters.

You show me this place

        where four-leaf clovers aren't so rare.

You show me this place

        where (gum)trees still offer shade.

You show me this place

        where hills & clouds form backgrounds.

You show me this place

        where cars & canines can't go.

You show me this place

        where hardly any human beings tread.

You show me this place

        where white-bellied sea eagles

                        soar.

You show me this place

        where the magpies don't swoop

                        us.

You show me this place

        where the kookaburras come so close.

You show me this place

        where the birdsongs seem quite unique.

You show me this place

        where traditional tunes were once sung.

You show me this place

        where we recall revived folk songs.

You show me this place

        where your soft voice

                resonates.

You show me this place

        where you walk/run/rest/swim in such peace.

You show me this place

        where we embrace.

You show me this place.

        Where?

Acknowledgements

The poems in this collection were written across two locations: the unceded lands of the Dja Dja Wurrung people and the unceded lands of the Awabakal people. I acknowledge the Traditional Custodians of these lands and pay my respects to their Elders past, present, and emerging.

'Blue Thought' won the UniSA Mental Health and Wellbeing Competition (2015) while 'Emergence of Voice' jointly won the the poetry category of the Minds Shine Bright Confidence Writing Competition (2022), alongside 'Dahlias' by Welsh poet Kevin Dyer. 'Acoustics' was longlisted in the poetry category of the Minds Shine Bright Confidence Writing Competition (2023) and longlisted in the University of Canberra Health Poetry Prize (2024). 'I Recall When the Kind ICU Staff Kept Calm' received a commendation in the FPM-Hippocrates Health Professional Prize for Poetry and Medicine (UK, 2021). 'Plight of the Adélie Penguin' was a finalist in the Antarctic Poetry Exhibition Competition (2019).

Certain poems in this collection first appeared (some in earlier forms or under different titles) in the following journals, websites, anthologies and exhibitions:

The Miramichi Reader (Canada), *Confidence: Minds Shine Bright Anthology* 2022 (Minds Shine Bright, 2022), *Friday Flash Fiction* (UK), *Chronicity* (Melbourne Poets Union, 2020), *Spillwords* (US), *Otoliths, Stereo Stories, Farrago, Visual Verse* (Germany), *Medical Humanities* (US and UK), *Live Encounters* (Indonesia), *Mindshare, Rural Fiction Magazine* (US), *Meniscus Literary Journal, The Sound of a Single Wave: Responses to Paintings by Andrew Bennett* (WordXimage, 9 to 27 September

2023), *Finding My Feet Anthology: An Anthology of Poetic Voices* (Melbourne Poets Union, 2023), *Close Up: Poems on Cancer, Grief, Hope, and Healing* (Orchard Lea Books, 2022), *The 2021 Hippocrates Prize Anthology of Winning and Commended Poems* (The Hippocrates Press, US, 2021), *Pulse – Voices from the Heart of Medicine* (US), *Family, Systems & Health* (US), *under the same moon: Fourth Australian Haiku Anthology* (Forty South Publishing Pty Ltd, 2024), *Lockdown Poetry: The Covid Long Haul* (Liquid Amber Press, 2021), *Poetry d'Amour 2024: Love Poems Selected by Shey Marque* (WA Poets, Inc., 2024), *In Telescope Time…Poetry at the Pub Anthology 2024* (Poetry at the Pub, 2024), *Harmony Magazine* (US), *Antarctic Poetry Exhibition, Rural Ecologies* (In Case of Emergency Press, 2024), *Poetry d'Amour 2022: Love Poems* (WA Poets, Inc., 2022) and *Co.Lab Exhibition 2023* (Dudley House, Bendigo, August to September 2023).

I am grateful to all of the editors, judges and curators who published, awarded or exhibited poems featured in this collection. In particular, my thanks to Vin Maskell – the founding editor of music and memoir website *Stereo Stories* – for believing in my nonfiction poems about music and for kindly referring to me as the 'resident poet' at *Stereo Stories*.

To my beloved family and partner, Irina, thank you for always supporting me in whatever I choose to do. I love you all so very much.

About the Author

Michael J. Leach (@m_jleach) is an Australian poet, critic and academic who works at the Monash University School of Rural Health. Michael's poems have appeared in journals such as *Cordite* and *Plumwood Mountain*, exhibitions such as the City of Greater Bendigo's *Co.Lab exhibitions*, anthologies such as annual editions of *The Best Australian Science Writing* (NewSouth Publishing, 2024 and 2025), and his three previously published poetry books: the chapbook *Chronicity* (Melbourne Poets Union, 2020), the full-length collection *Natural Philosophies* (Recent Work Press, 2022), and a haiku and senryu collection titled *Rural Ecologies* (In Case of Emergency Press, 2024). Michael has performed poetry at various events, conferences and festivals, including performing his poem about 'Over the Rainbow' with musical backing during the *Stereo Stories* concert at Bendigo Writers Festival (2021). Michael's poems have been recognised in competitions: first place in the UniSA Mental Health and Wellbeing Poetry Competition (2015), commended in the Hippocrates Prize for Poetry and Medicine (2021), joint first place in the poetry category of the Minds Shine Bright Confidence Writing Competition (2022), longlisted in the poetry category of the Minds Shine Bright Confidence Writing Competition (2023), shortlisted in the poetry category of the Woollahra Digital Literary Award (2023), highly commended and longlisted in the Liquid Amber Poetry Prize (2024), longlisted in the University of Canberra Health Poetry Prize (2024), and highly commended in the Hush Foundation Kindness in Healthcare Writing Prize (2024). He lives on unceded Dja Dja Wurrung Country and acknowledges the Traditional Custodians of the land.